D1302731

Steve Parish

CELEBRATING AUSTRALIA

CANBERRA

Steve Parish
PUBLISHING

Previous pages: Canberra at dusk, seen from Mt Ainslie.

Above: Capital Hill crowned by Parliament House and the land axis running to distant Mt Ainslie.

Introduction

Canberra is a marvellous place to visit, for all its sights are so logically positioned and so well spaced. It was founded in 1913 and followed a plan created by landscape architect Walter Burley Griffin, whose vision was of a spacious city, in which it was possible to travel in a short time between any two places.

Burley Griffin designed a Canberra balanced along a land axis running from Bimberi Peak through Red Hill and Capital Hill, across the waterway which he foresaw would result from the damming of the Molonglo River, then up Anzac Parade to the Australian War Memorial and Mt Ainslie. He sited the buildings to house the great federal institutions, Parliament House and the High Court of Australia, in the "Parliamentary Triangle". Today, with the National Library, the National Gallery and the National Science and Technology Centre, they stand in close proximity to the magnificent lake which was finally created in 1963 and named after its far-sighted planner.

The proximity of all these superb buildings, their positions on the scenic shores of Lake Burley Griffin and the wise planting which has turned Canberra into a garden city add up to a photographer's delight. Like many other visitors, I particularly enjoy the visual contrast of Canberra's seasons: the fiery leaves of autumn give way to winter's bare branches and cool evergreens, before spring brings new foliage and a splendour of flowers, which usher in the warm blues skies and lazy golden days of summer. Floriade, Canberra's annual celebration of flowers, attracts enthusiast visitors each September.

Over half of all Canberra is reserved for open spaces for public use. It is one of the world's loveliest cities, a worthy national capital for Australia.

Steve Parish

Canberra – a planned city

The design of Canberra, Australia's national capital situated in the Australian Capital Territory, resulted from a world-wide competition announced in 1911. When the first survey peg was driven into the ground in 1913, the wife of the Governor-General, Lady Denman, announced that the city would be named Canberra, derived from the Aboriginal word "canberry," meaning a meeting place.

The Federation of the States of Australia in 1901 brought the need for a common meeting place and a site for federal institutions. After considerable rivalry between Melbourne and Sydney, a location midway between these two State capitals was chosen. The Commonwealth of Australia officially assumed control of the Australian Capital Territory on 1 January 1911.

Canberra was founded in 1913 and became one of the world's very few planned cities, designed to serve as a seat of federal government and a location for the embassies and high commissions of other nations' governments.

Left: Canberra City and Lake Burley Griffin.

Parliament House

Parliament House, which occupies Capital Hill, was opened on 9 May 1988 and was designed by Mitchell/Giurgola & Thorp Architects. The building is surmounted by a flag mast 81 metres high, one of the world's largest stainless steel structures and a Canberra landmark in its own right.

The impressive Forecourt mosaic, which is such a feature of the approach to Parliament House, is based on a design by Aboriginal artist Michael Tjakamarra Nelson. Made up of 100 000 pieces of granite, it represents a meeting place, and stands within the Forecourt pool on an island which symbolises the continent of Australia.

Left: A striking mosaic forms a foreground to the Great Verandah and Parliament House Entrance.
Following pages: The House of Representatives Chamber on the eastern side of Parliament House is decorated in shades of green; the Senate Chamber on the western side features burgundy tonings.

No public
access

The interior of Parliament House

The Foyer of Parliament House.

The magnificent Foyer of Parliament House features forty-eight marble-clad columns and two superb marble staircases. This breath-taking entrance is intended to remind its viewers of a eucalypt forest. On the walls are paintings representing the arrival of Europeans on the continent. Guided tours allow inspection of Parliament House, or visitors may discover the building's wonders at their leisure.

The Main Committee Room, Parliament House.

The Senate, the Upper House of the Australian Federal Parliament, appoints committees to enquire into matters of public concern and to inspect proposed legislation. Such a committee is made up of equal numbers of government and non-government senators. Members of the public may take their ideas, information and grievances directly to these committees and their activities are widely advertised.

Above: A painting showing the opening of Parliament House in 1988.

Above: Tom Roberts's painting showing the opening of Old Parliament House in 1927.
Opposite: The Great Hall, Parliament House.

Historic splendour

The transitional building known today as Old Parliament House served from 1927 until 1988, when the present Parliament House was opened by HRH Queen Elizabeth II. The paintings showing these ceremonies are part of the Parliament House Art Collection, which expresses the diversity of Australian culture and includes more than 3000 works. The Historic Memorials Collection is made up of portraits, while the Gift Collection consists of presented works. The centrepiece of the Great Hall, shown opposite, is an enormous tapestry designed by Arthur Boyd and woven by the Victorian Tapestry Workshop.

Areas for relaxation

Above: Admiring a statue on Queens Terrace.   *Opposite:* Courtyards provide open space in the interior of the massive building.

Parliament House includes a number of courtyards and other areas where the public and resident workers can relax and refresh themselves. The Queens Terrace Cafe is on the first floor: striking sculptures decorate both the terrace, which overlooks the building's entrance, and the various courtyards within the complex.

Parliament House is open to the public seven days a week between 9 a.m. and 5 p.m., with the exception of Christmas Day.

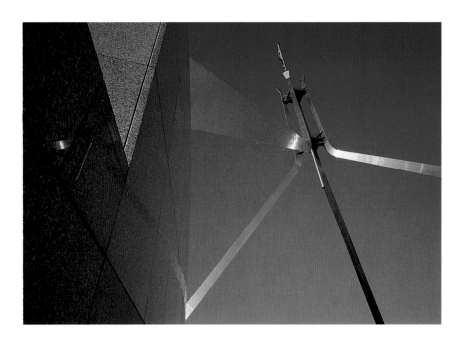

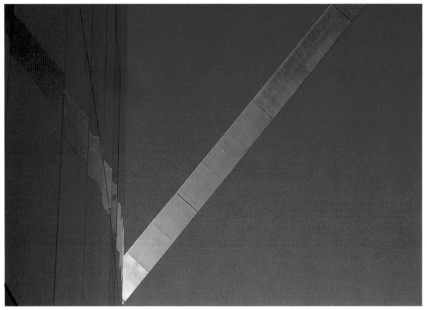

Top and above: Two views of the flag mast, Parliament House.
Preceding pages: Looking out from the Great Verandah to distant Mt Ainslie.

A nation's showplace

Parliament House dominates, yet does not stand above, Capital Hill. The main visible elements of the massive structure are the eastern and western wings, enormous curving walls, grassed walkway and elegant flag mast. They complement, and do not interrupt, the plans of Canberra's designer, which required a land axis with a line of vision to be established from Bimberi Peak on one side of the city to Mt Ainslie on the other.

Above: Parliament House, Canberra.

Following pages: The transitional (Old) Parliament House was in use by Parliament from 1927 to 1988.

Old Parliament House

Old Parliament House at night.

For 51 years, the building shown above served as the seat of Federal Parliaments. Today, a gracious building set amongst lawns, trees and rose gardens, it is used for historic displays, conferences and social functions.

Old Parliament House in the foreground, with the present Parliament House behind it.

Festive Canberra

The middle of March each year brings the ten-day Canberra Festival, which attracts more than 200 000 people to celebrate the founding of the National Capital. Concerts in the parks, a parade, an outdoor art exhibition, the outrageous Birdman Rally and the fireworks of Skyfire are outstanding attractions.

However, the trademarks of this annual birthday celebration are the multicoloured balloons which take off from the Parliamentary foreshore at dawn and soar buoyantly over Canberra, carrying enthralled passengers to view the sights of the city from the air.

Left: Balloons float over Lake Burley Griffin, past the National Library.

Inside the National Library.

Opposite: The National Library of Australia.   *Above:* Stained glass windows in the National Library.

The National Library

Standing on the shores of Lake Burley Griffin, the National Library of Australia houses a fine collection of books. It also contains pictorial material of all kinds, archives, newspapers and journals, maps, manuscripts and films. It has a fine collection of unique oral history recordings.

For those exhausted by learning, or simply wishing to take refreshment in relaxing surroundings, there is a bistro and an excellent restaurant. The Library Shop specialises in Australian books, and displays can be viewed in the Visitor Centre and Exhibition Centre.

Lake Burley Griffin

Lake Burley Griffin was formed after the flow of water along the Molonglo River was impeded by the construction of Scrivener Dam. Its appearance, in 1964, was a realisation of the inspired plan of Canberra's designer, Walter Burley Griffin.

Besides being a major ornamental feature of the city, this spectacular stretch of water is used for fishing and a variety of aquatic sports. Its 35 kilometres of foreshore are ringed with cycle and walking tracks and with parks which serve as picnic and barbecue spots. Cruises, boat and cycle hire operate from the terminal at Acton.

Left: The Captain Cook Terrestrial Globe stands on Lake Burley Griffin's Regatta Point, bedecked with spring blossom, opposite the Australian National Library.

The Captain Cook Memorial Water Jet, seen over the globe which traces Cook's three great voyages.

The Captain Cook Memorial Water Jet

The Captain Cook Memorial Water Jet in Lake Burley Griffin sends a six-tonne column of water into the air from 10 a.m. to noon, 2 to 4 p.m. and 7 to 9 p.m. during daylight saving time. This spectacular cascade and the Terrestrial Globe on nearby Regatta Point pay tribute to the great navigator whose three voyages opened up so much of the Pacific Ocean for Britain.

Opposite: The Captain Cook Memorial Water Jet, with the Telstra Tower on Black Mountain silhouetted in the background.

The High Court of Australia

The High Court of Australia stands on Lake Burley Griffin.

The interior of the High Court makes extensive use of native timbers.

The highest court in Australia's judicial system first sat in 1903, and became established in the present magnificent building on the shores of Lake Burley Griffin in 1980. The High Court building is 40 metres in height and contains a public hall, three courtrooms, an administration wing and rooms for the seven Justices of the Court.

Opposite: Cascades border the steps leading to the High Court's entrance.

Australian National Gallery

Top and above: Inside the Australian National Gallery.
Opposite: The Australian National Gallery at night.

The Australian National Gallery

Opened in 1982, the Australian National Gallery houses Australian art ranging from traditional Aboriginal art through works from the early days of European settlement to modern artists. The Gallery's extensive collections include works from other countries, ages and cultures, as well as works on paper of all kinds, photographs, furniture, textiles and ceramics. Sculpture is displayed indoors and outdoors in the Sculpture Garden.

Opposite: The Australian National Gallery by day.

Above: Sculptures displayed in the Sculpture Garden and surrounds of the National Gallery.

35

Above: Questacon visitors can use their bodies and minds to unlock the mysteries of science.
Opposite: Sculpture outside Questacon (the National Science and Technology Centre).

Questacon

At the National Science and Technology Centre, otherwise known as Questacon, members of the public can explore science and technology in a variety of hands-on exhibits. Entrance is via a sweeping ramp, which takes the visitor to the top of the Drum, the 27 metre high tower which dominates the complex. From here, a spiral ramp leads to five galleries full of fascinating displays, where pushing, pulling, playing and asking questions are encouraged.

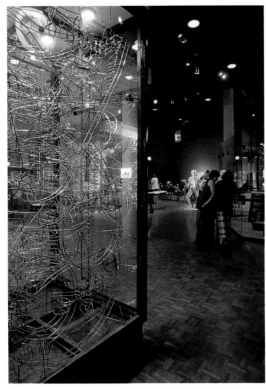

Opposite: Questacon's Drum Tower, seen at night.

Above: Exhibits at Questacon.

The Royal Australian Mint

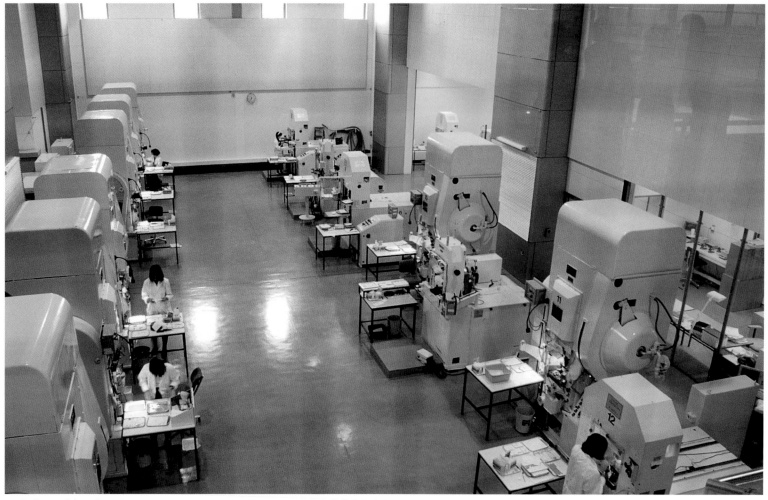

Inside the Royal Australian Mint.

The Royal Australian Mint, in Deakin, south of Lake Burley Griffin, introduces visitors to the manufacturing of Australian currency with an extensive display of rare coins. The entire process of minting money, from raw materials to finished coins, can be viewed through plate-glass windows and visitors can even make their own coin or token.

The Treasury Building

The lights of the Treasury Building mirrored in the pool in the forecourt.

The Department of the Treasury and the Department of Finance are housed in Parkes. In this building, the economic fate of the nation is shaped: its public servants advise the Treasurer and the government on broad economic policy and the day-to-day economics of government expenditure and revenue.

The Australian War Memorial

Above: Stained glass windows in the Hall of Memory, Australian War Memorial.

Above: In the Tomb of the Unknown Soldier lies an Australian who died in World War I.
Opposite: The Australian War Memorial is in the shape of a cross.

Anzac Parade, which leads to the Australian War Memorial at the foot of Mt Ainslie, is bordered by a number of memorials to campaigns in which Australians have taken part. The War Memorial itself, which was opened in 1941, houses relics of conflict and other memorabilia. In the focus of the complex, the Hall of Memory, lies the body of Australia's Unknown Soldier, brought from a World War I battlefield.

Above: The entrance to the domed War Memorial and Museum.

Lest the people forget

Above: Simpson, his donkey and a wounded soldier, commemorated in bronze.

The front entrance of the Australian War Memorial, which also serves as a military museum, faces directly down Anzac Parade to Old Parliament House across Lake Burley Griffin. It is thus on the land axis visualised by Canberra's designer and forms a point of pilgrimage for most visitors to the National Capital. Whatever their feelings about warfare, or their nationality, they cannot fail to be impressed by the dignified building and its solemn atmosphere. The representation in bronze of the gallant Simpson and his commandeered donkey carrying a wounded soldier to safety in the hellhole that was Gallipoli, an action repeated until Simpson himself was killed, has touched the hearts of many.

Following pages: Three views along Walter Burley Griffin's land axis.

The embassies

There are between 60 and 70 embassies and high commissions in Canberra. Some of the most interesting architectural designs include the tiled Chinese Embassy, the temple-style Thai Embassy, the US Embassy which resembles a Southern mansion, and Papua New Guinea's facsimile of a spirit-house from the Sepik region. Several times each year, a number of embassies open their doors to the public.

Left: An aerial view of various embassies; Parliament House is at top right and Lotus Bay on Lake Burley Griffin is at bottom right.

The Embassy of Brazil.

The Embassy of Greece.

The Embassy of China.

The High Commission of Papua New Guinea.

The High Commission of India.

The High Commission of Singapore.

The Embassy of Ireland.

The Embassy of the Union of Myanmar.

The Embassy of Japan.

The Embassy of Spain.

The High Commission of Malaysia.

The High Commission of Canada.

Interior of St John the Baptist Church.

St John the Baptist Church, with its leaning spire.

The Church of
St John the Baptist

The foundation stone of the church of St John the Baptist, on Constitution Avenue, was laid in May 1841. It was named after the prophet who preached in the wilderness. The land was donated by Robert Campbell and the Australian-made stained glass window above the altar bears the Campbell family crest and motto, *Agite pro viribus* (work with all your might). The original sandstone tower was struck by lightning and demolished in 1864. Its replacement was completed in 1878 after great difficulties and has a definite tilt to one side.

Above: Bruce Hall, Australian National University.

Above: In the grounds of the Australian National University.
Opposite: The Academy of Science building, Australian National University.

The Australian National University

Located on 145 hectares between Civic and Black Mountain on the shores of Lake Burley Griffin, the Australian National University offers the highest standards of academic and practical education in gracious surroundings. It grew from the Canberra University College, established in 1931 and originally attached to the University of Melbourne, but is now a highly respected institute of learning which attracts students from all over Australia and South-East Asia.

Built to endure

The Calthorpe family's house and garden exemplifies the period between the World Wars.

The Calthorpes' house at Mugga Way, Red Hill, was built in 1927 and was purchased by the Commonwealth in 1984 for the National Estate. It records an age when buildings, appliances and furnishings were intended to last rather than become quickly obsolete, and preserves the values, fashions, technology and social roles of the period 1927 to 1945.

Blundells Farmhouse in Wendouree Drive, Parkes.

In about 1860, the Campbell family completed a stone cottage to house Duntroon's chief ploughman, William Ginn, his wife Mary and their four children. The next occupants were bullock driver George Blundell, his wife Mary, who was the district's midwife, and their eight children. Blundell descendants lived in the cottage for the next 50 years.

Monuments in stone

Convict-built Duntroon is now the Officers' Mess of the Royal Military College.

In 1825, Sydney merchant Robert Campbell was awarded a grant of land which included Mt Ainslie and the present-day suburb of Reid. Eight years later, the house first known as Limestone Cottage, and now as Duntroon, had been built. Its walls are 91 centimetres thick, hewn from local rock by convicts who made the three-week trek from Sydney.

Lanyon, an historic property 30 kilometres south of Canberra.

Lanyon homestead complex and the nearby gallery featuring the paintings of Sydney Nolan (including many of the Ned Kelly series), are administered by the Museums Unit of the ACT Government. The surrounding area is a working cattle and sheep property, whose landscape reflects over 150 years of European pastoral enterprise.

The Australian Institute of Sport

Above: The Australian Institute of Sport.   *Opposite and following pages:* Some of the striking sculptures in the grounds of the Institute.

Australians have always admired sporting prowess and, in a bid to ensure success on international playing fields, the Australian Institute of Sport was established in 1981. The AIS provides facilities for the training and coaching of Australia's best young athletes, and is at the leading edge of sports science and sports medicine. Visitors can participate in a hands-on sports exhibition – Sportex – and be guided around the AIS site by one of Australia's promising young sports stars.

64

A reconstruction of an Australian dinosaur.

One of the displays at the National Dinosaur Museum.

National Dinosaur Museum

The National Dinosaur Museum is located at Gold Creek Village, in Gungahlin. Its more than 300 exhibits include full-size replica skeletons of dinosaurs, plus enormous bones and skulls and life-sized reconstructions of a number of Australian dinosaurs. The history of life on Earth is illustrated by many finely detailed replicas of fossils prepared by Mike Durrant, founder/curator of the Museum.

Visitors can view aquatic life from a walk-through tunnel.

A scuba diver working in one of the displays.

The National Aquarium

Australia's coastline is over 36 000 kilometres in length and the country's residents, and most of the visitors to its shores, have a fascination with the sea and marine life. The National Aquarium, near Scrivener Dam at the western edge of Lake Burley Griffin, features underwater creatures from salt and fresh water, and offers an impressive walk-through viewing tunnel. It is surrounded by an extensive wildlife sanctuary.

City by a lake

Dawn lights Lake Burley Griffin.

Opposite: Twilight falls on the lake.

Walter Burley Griffin did not live to see his vision of Canberra standing on its stately lake realised, but since 1964 this magnificent expanse of water has been one of Canberra's chief beauties.

The lake is 11 kilometres in length and its landscaped surrounds form scenic recreational areas, while its waters are a year-round playground.

Opposite, above and top: The beauty of Lake Burley Griffin.

Evening light, Lake Burley Griffin.

The Australian-American Memorial rises above the morning mist.

Sculling on Lake Burley Griffin at dawn.

Fun in the sun

Feeding the gulls and waterfowl which live around Lake Burley Griffin.

Seeing the sights on a bicycle built for two.

Racing dragon boats on the lake.

Sailing for pleasure, with Kings Avenue Bridge in the background.

Although Canberra can be cold in winter, sunny days allow plenty of scope for outdoor activities. In summer, fun in the sun generally focuses on the cool expanses of Lake Burley Griffin or its surrounding parklands and tracks.

Opposite: Hot-air balloons take off from the Parliamentary Foreshore.

The Carillon

In 1963, Great Britain presented a bell tower, the Carillon, to Canberra to celebrate the city's fiftieth anniversary. This splendid birthday gift, which stands on Aspen Island near Kings Avenue Bridge, contains 53 bells, whose weights range from 7 kilograms to 6 tonnes.

Peals are rung on Wednesdays from 12.45 to 1.30 p.m., and on weekends and public holidays from 2.45 to 3.30 p.m.

Left and opposite: The Carillon on Aspen Island.

Autumn splendour

Above and opposite: Canberra's deciduous trees don their autumn colours.

Canberra has been planted with a variety of Northern Hemisphere trees. As the first chills of autumn arrive, deciduous trees prepare to drop their leaves, which change to shades of bronze, russet and gold. The native and exotic evergreens, with their silvery-green and forest-green foliage, form a charming background to this blaze of fiery colours.

A peaceful autumn scene on the bank of Nerang Pool.

Russet and gold leaves and the silver Captain Cook Memorial Water Jet reflected in Nerang Pool.

Above and opposite: The golden glory of autumn poplars around Lake Burley Griffin.

Floriade

The spectacular festival of blossom which is Canberra's Floriade turns Commonwealth Park into a blaze of colour from mid-September to mid-October each year, entrancing half a million visitors.

Floriade involves the whole Canberra community and blends floral display with cultural events, outdoor entertainments and other happenings. Each year brings new designs and innovative themes for the glorious beds of bulbs and annuals and the events which accompany their display.

Left and following pages: Floriade brings colourful carpets of flowers to Canberra's Commonwealth Park.

Above: This bust of Sir Joseph Banks, who travelled with Captain Cook to Australia, stands in the gardens.
Opposite: The Rainforest Walk is a popular attraction.

The Australian National Botanic Gardens

The Australian National Botanic Gardens occupy a 50-hectare site on the slopes of Black Mountain. Plants from all parts of Australia are displayed for visitors and are used for research into plant classification and biology. The Rainforest Walk, the Aboriginal Trail and the Rock Garden are particularly popular with visitors. The herbarium houses a collection of specimens used for scientific research. The first trees in the gardens were planted in 1949 and the complex was opened to the public in 1970.

The Telstra Tower

Above: The Telstra Tower stands tall on Black Mountain.

Opposite and following pages: Views of the Telstra Tower.

Black Mountain rises 812 metres above the plains on which Canberra stands, and is dominated by the Telstra Tower which is 195 metres tall. This imposing spire houses a display covering the history of communications in Australia, and three levels of state of the art equipment that provides vital telecommunications links for the whole country.

From the revolving restaurant, diners can enjoy panoramic views of Canberra and its surroundings. Several viewing platforms allow sightseeing and photography — public access is invited from 9 a.m. to 10 p.m. every day of the year.

Civic

Preceding pages: The city of Canberra.

Above and opposite: Civic.

Canberra, the planned city, has a clear separation of commercial centres from museums, galleries, law courts and civic authorities. Civic, where most of the everyday business of life is conducted, is on the northern side of Lake Burley Griffin, centred on Vernon Circle. It contains bus terminals, banks, the general Post Office and pedestrian shopping malls, as well as theatres, a casino and other places of entertainment. The main road north of the lake, Northbourne Avenue, is flanked by the Melbourne and Sydney Buildings, which are replicas of each other.

The Times Fountain, in Civic's centre, was presented to the city by the *Canberra Times* newspaper.

Casino Canberra, in Binara Street, describes itself as "a boutique-style casino".

Civic is distinguished by wide streets and green, shaded, public areas.

Civic is the commercial heart of Canberra.

Canberra's suburbs

Above: The interior of Belconnen Shopping Centre.

Canberra's suburbs have been carefully planned to include house blocks of all types and sizes. The aim has been to prevent the development of privileged or less privileged areas, and, accompanied by a decentralisation policy, it has worked extremely well.

Belconnen is a good example of an urban area where the Australian dream of house ownership is realised by many residents, and where excellent schools, shops, sports areas and other facilities are within easy reach of all. Of course, few suburbs anywhere in the world enjoy Belconnen's superb location, in proximity to scenic Lake Ginninderra, an artificial lake one-seventh the size of Lake Burley Griffin.

Right: An aerial view of Belconnen and Lake Ginninderra.

Cockington Green

An English village in miniature at Cockington Green.

Cockington Green is a display of miniature British buildings set amidst lovely gardens, located at Gold Creek Road, Gungahlin. The replicas are one-twelfth scale and each model is an accurate reproduction of a traditional Old World construction. Visitors can dine at the Parsons Nose Restaurant, or ride on a miniature steam train.

Above and above right: Visitors stroll amongst mini-landscapes at Cockington Green.

The view from Mt Ainslie

Above: Mt Ainslie offers many vantage points.

Opposite: A view of Canberra from Mt Ainslie.

There are a number of vantage points from which Canberra and the country around it can be appreciated. Black Mountain and the Telstra Tower, Red Hill (which rises to 722 metres above sea level), Mt Pleasant (665 metres) which is approached through the grounds of the Royal Military College, and Mt Ainslie (842 metres) are the best known of these.

Mt Ainslie, on the north-eastern side of the city of Canberra is reached by road or by walking tracks. It offers a fine view of the city, the Parliamentary Triangle and Lake Burley Griffin.

Bushland clothes the slopes of Mt Ainslie.

The magic hour between dusk and darkness.

Tidbinbilla

Tidbinbilla Nature Reserve is surrounded by the Tidbinbilla Range.

Tidbinbilla Nature Reserve is 40 kilometres south-west of Canberra, in mountainous surroundings. Here Australia's native animals can be observed in their natural habitat: groups of kangaroos usually find plenty of good grazing, Koalas may be discovered in forested areas, and Emus regularly invite themselves to join picnics and barbecues.

Above: The Deep Space Communication Complex, Tidbinbilla.

Pages 110, 111: Wildlife at Tidbinbilla — Koala and Eastern Grey Kangaroo.
Pages 112, 113: Canberra from Red Hill.

Tidbinbilla Deep Space Communication Complex is operated by the Australian Department of Science for the US National Aeronautics and Space Administration. It is one of three tracking stations maintained by NASA world-wide. Visitors can view displays of spacecraft and tracking technology and learn about space exploration.

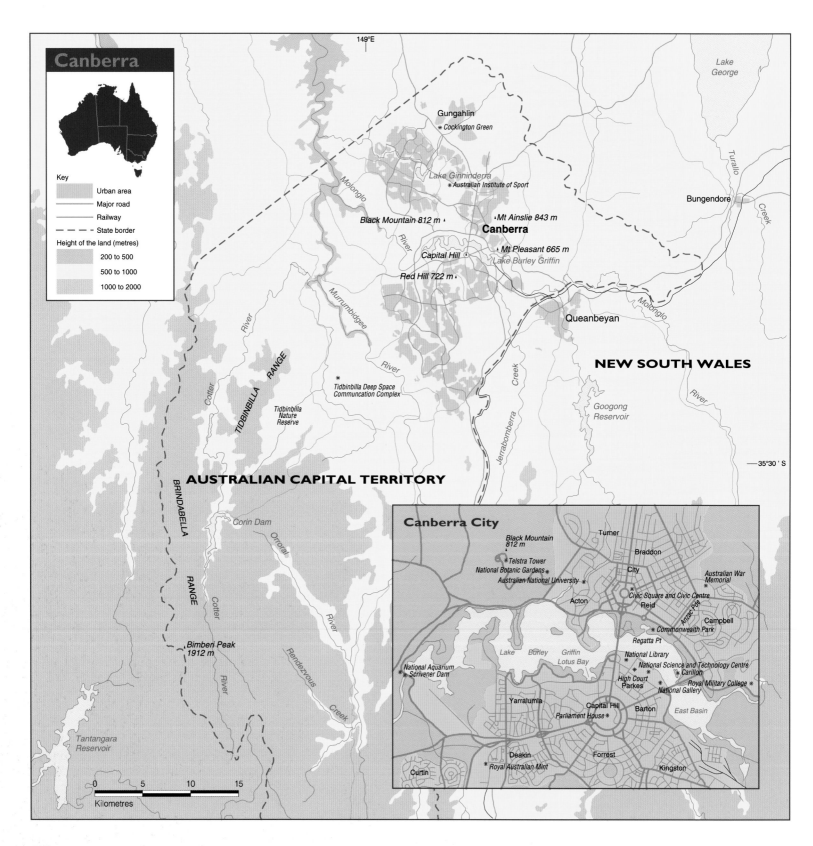

Canberra

Key
- Urban area
- Major road
- Railway
- State border

Height of the land (metres)
- 200 to 500
- 500 to 1000
- 1000 to 2000

Gungahlin
* Cockington Green

Lake Ginninderra
* Australian Institute of Sport

Black Mountain 812 m ▲

Mt Ainslie 843 m ▲

Canberra

Molonglo River

Mt Pleasant 665 m ▲

Capital Hill

Lake Burley Griffin

Red Hill 722 m ▲

Murrumbidgee River

Queanbeyan

Molonglo

NEW SOUTH WALES

TIDBINBILLA RANGE

* Tidbinbilla Deep Space
Communcation Complex

Tidbinbilla
Nature
Reserve

Cotter River

Jerrabomberra Creek

Googong
Reservoir

Lake George

Turallo Creek

Bungendore

River

— 35°30 ' S

BRINDABELLA RANGE

AUSTRALIAN CAPITAL TERRITORY

Corin Dam

Orroral

Cotter River

Bimberi Peak
1912 m

Rendezvous Creek

Tantangara
Reservoir

0   5   10   15
Kilometres

Canberra City

Black Mountain
812 m

* Telstra Tower
National Botanic Gardens *
Australian National University *

Acton

Turner

Braddon

City

Australian War
Memorial

* Civic Square and Civic Centre
Reid

Campbell

* Commonwealth Park

Regatta Pt

Lake   Burley   Griffin
Lotus Bay

National Library

* National Science and Technology Centre
* Carillon

* National Aquarium
* Scrivener Dam

High Court
Parkes

Royal Military College *
* National Gallery

Yarralumla

Capital Hill
Parliament House *

Barton

East Basin

Deakin

Forrest

Kingston

Curtin

* Royal Australian Mint

149°E

149°E

The Australian flag flies proudly over Canberra.

Australia's Coat of Arms, with kangaroo, emu, wattle blossom and six State symbols.

Canberra on parade

Canberra is a city in which it is easy to be a proud Australian. Visitors from other nations find in Canberra an appreciation of Australia's virtues and a spirit of friendliness that bridges cultural gaps.

Australia's National Capital blends Australian ways and customs, architecture and landscapes with those of other lands. From its carefully planned beginnings through its nearly one hundred years of growth, its architects, its politicians, its diplomats and its residents have melded the best from many cultures with uniquely Australian elements.

Canberra's gardens are a fine example of this. The use of native and exotic plants has produced magnificent civic and suburban landscapes. Remove either element and the green spaces of city and suburbs would be immeasurably the poorer.

So Canberra is a multicultural city, where Australia and the world meet in a place which is remarkable for its beauty, its planned spaciousness and its gracious, welcoming atmosphere.

Steve Parish

World-famous photographer Steve Parish began his remarkable career by recording marine life off Australia's coasts. After discovering the fascinations of the rainforest and its wild creatures, he has spent much of his life journeying around Australia photographing the landscapes, plants, animals and the people of the land. Of recent years, he has extended the range of his subjects to include Australia's cities and towns.

The magnificent library of images which has resulted has become the heart of Steve Parish Publishing Pty Ltd. Through the firm's publications, Steve and his wife and partner Jan are realising their dream of sharing Australia with the world.

Celebrating Australia is a collection of titles which present the incomparable beauty of the southern continent in superb photographs and text. As Steve comments: "After a lifetime of travel and asking questions, I have only just begun to discover how much there is to learn about Australia. I hope these books arouse in others a desire like mine to explore and to appreciate this wonderful country."

Index

First published by Steve Parish Publishing Pty Ltd, 1997
PO Box 2160, Fortitude Valley BC, Queensland 4006, Australia

© copyright Steve Parish Publishing Pty Ltd, 1997

ISBN 1 875932 96 8

Photography: Steve Parish
Text: Pat Slater, Steve Parish Publishing, Australia

All rights reserved. No part of this publication may be reproduced, stored in a retrieval system, transmitted in any form or by any means, electronic, mechanical, photocopying, recording or otherwise without the prior permission in writing of the Publisher.

Map supplied by MAPgraphics
Editing, design: Steve Parish Publishing, Australia
Printed in Hong Kong
Colour separations by Steve Parish Publishing, Australia